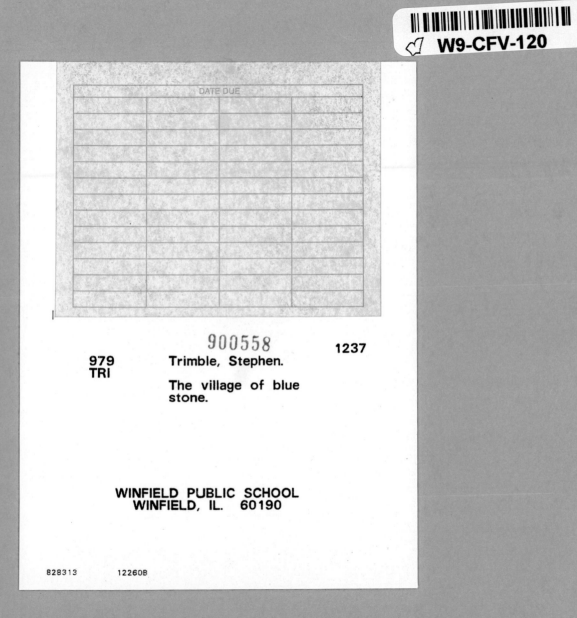

THE VILLAGE OF BLUE STONE

▲▲▲▲▲▲▲▲▲▲▲▲▲▲▲▲▲▲▲▲▲▲▲▲▲▲

THE VILLAGE OF BLUE STONE

▲▲▲

WORDS BY
STEPHEN TRIMBLE

ILLUSTRATIONS BY
JENNIFER OWINGS DEWEY
AND
DEBORAH READE

MACMILLAN PUBLISHING COMPANY   NEW YORK
COLLIER MACMILLAN PUBLISHERS   LONDON

FOR JOANNE AND DORY

—S.T.

TO MY FAMILY

—D.R.

▲▲▲

For their help in checking the accuracy of the archaeology, I thank Linda Cordell, California Academy of Sciences; Jonathan Haas, School of American Research; and Stephen Lekson, Arizona State Museum. Any remaining errors are my own.

First Edition. Printed in the United States of America.   10   9   8   7   6   5   4   3   2   1

The text of this book is set in 12 point Egyptian 505. The illustrations are rendered in pencil.

Library of Congress Cataloging-in-Publication Data
Trimble, Stephen, date. The village of blue stone.
Bibliography: p.   Includes index.
Summary: Re-creates, in text and illustrations, the day-to-day life throughout a full year in a Chaco Culture Anasazi pueblo, located in what is now New Mexico, in 1100 A.D. 1. Pueblo Indians — Social life and customs — Juvenile literature. 2. Indians of North America — Southwest, New — Social life and customs — Juvenile literature. 3. Cliff-dwellings — Southwest, New — Juvenile literature. 4. Mesa Verde National Park (Colo.) — Juvenile literature. [1. Pueblo Indians — Social life and customs. 2. Indians of North America — Southwest, New — Social life and customs. 3. Cliff dwellings — Colorado. 4. Mesa Verde National Park (Colo.)] I. Dewey, Jennifer, ill. II. Reade, Deborah, ill. III. Title.
E99.P9T76   1990   979'.01   88-34194
ISBN 0-02-789501-7

CONTENTS

▲ ▲ ▲ ▲ ▲ ▲

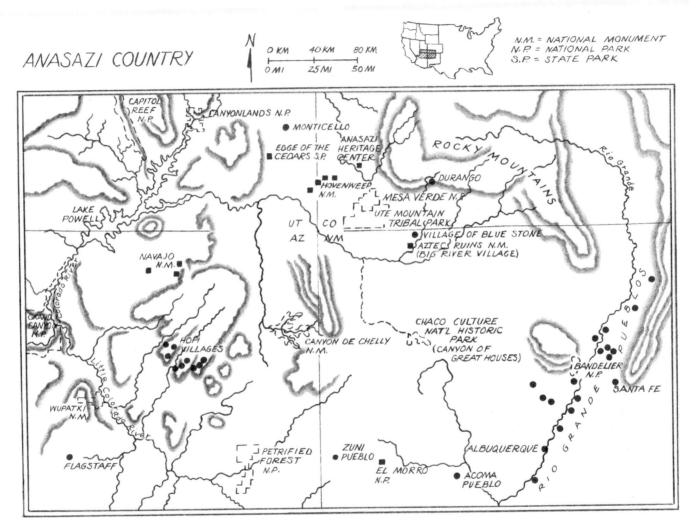

ANASAZI COUNTRY

N

| 0 KM | 40 KM | 80 KM |
| 0 MI | 25 MI | 50 MI |

N.M. = NATIONAL MONUMENT
N.P. = NATIONAL PARK
S.P. = STATE PARK

CAPITOL REEF N.P.

CANYONLANDS N.P.

MONTICELLO

EDGE OF THE CEDARS S.P.

ANASAZI HERITAGE CENTER

ROCKY MOUNTAINS

Rio Grande

HOVENWEEP N.M.

DURANGO

MESA VERDE N.P.

UTE MOUNTAIN TRIBAL PARK

LAKE POWELL

UT CO

AZ NM

VILLAGE OF BLUE STONE

AZTEC RUINS N.M.
(BIG RIVER VILLAGE)

NAVAJO N.M.

Colorado River

GRAND CANYON N.P.

HOPI VILLAGES

Little Colorado River

CANYON DE CHELLY N.M.

CHACO CULTURE NAT'L HISTORIC PARK
(CANYON OF GREAT HOUSES)

PUEBLOS

BANDELIER N.P.

SANTA FE

WUPATKI N.M.

FLAGSTAFF

PETRIFIED FOREST N.P.

ZUNI PUEBLO

EL MORRO N.P.

ALBUQUERQUE

ACOMA PUEBLO

RIO GRANDE

▲▲▲▲▲ **R**ichard Wetherill and Charlie Mason were cold and wet—and tired of looking for lost cows. Snow was falling hard, and it deepened as they rode through the olive green piñon and juniper trees not much taller than their horses. They were hoping to find those last cows soon.

Richard began to worry about missing a cliff and tumbling over the edge, so the two cowboys got off their horses and walked out to the rim of the canyon to look around. It was December 18, 1888. The young men stood at the edge of Cliff Canyon on the high flat top of

Mesa Verde in southwest Colorado. As they looked through the steam of their breath and the veil of falling snow, they hoped to see a stray cow or two sheltering in the canyon bottom.

What they saw instead was a village of stone lying still and quiet in an alcove under the cliff rim across from them. They were absolutely amazed. They moved quickly once they recovered their wits, scrambling down and across the canyon to see if they could find a way into the ruin.

Richard had four brothers (Charlie Mason

1

was their brother-in-law). All six of them were fascinated by Indian ruins. The Wetherills had seen small groups of ancient abandoned houses up here on previous trips, and a Ute Indian man named Acowitz had told them of other larger ones. But they had never seen a ruin as large as this new one. The village had towers three stories high and contained more than two hundred rooms. The Wetherills were the first non-Indians to see it and they gave the ruin its English name: Cliff Palace.

After discovering Cliff Palace and its neighboring ruins on Mesa Verde, the Wetherills began looking for other abandoned pueblos in the mesas and canyons up and down the San Juan River and its tributaries. They found hundreds of ruins and collected artifacts from many of them. Some ruins were almost as large as Cliff Palace. Many were small, with just a few rooms. Some perched high in the cliffs, while the low walls of others rose from the flat tops of mesas.

The builders of these stone villages abandoned them long before the Wetherills came to Colorado. Though just why they left their homes remains a mystery, they did not disappear. They simply moved to other parts of the Southwest. Their descendants, the Pueblo Indians of New Mexico and Arizona, live today in stone and adobe villages that look much like the prehistoric villages.

Other Indian people, the Navajos, now live below the abandoned pueblos. They moved into this country after the villagers were already gone. The Navajos call the ancient people who built the stone houses the *Anasazi*, a name we use today. In Navajo, this word means "someone's ancestors."

This is the story of one village of those ancestors. It describes what a year of life might have been like in an Anasazi pueblo when it was a living village, almost nine centuries ago.

The village is imaginary, but it resembles dozens of small mesa-top pueblos that surrounded many larger villages. It is easy to picture Richard Wetherill and his younger brother, John, finding this abandoned village one warm spring day in 1892. Imagine them digging in the windblown sand between the falling walls. On that very first morning John might have found a carved turquoise parrot an inch long, giving the brothers a good name for the ruin: Turquoise House.

In this village we have imagined, the Indian people carved animals and made earrings and necklaces from turquoise. For this skill, Anasazi people living along the Big River might have called this place the Village of Blue Stone.

THE VILLAGE OF BLUE STONE

▲▲▲

Icy crystals came swirling down from the sky. The Sun Watcher crouched against the cliff out of the snow, waiting. It was still dark. He hoped the clouds would lift when the Sun rose behind Three Fingers Butte. At dawn he needed a clear sky.

For weeks he had watched the beam of morning sunlight move across the wall of a special room in the village, a room with narrow windows cut to mark the changing path of the Sun. Every day the Sun rose a little farther south on the horizon. Every day he had watched the beam come streaming in the east window and move across the wall.

One-half moon ago the sunbeam passed its second-to-last niche in the shrine room. He had counted the days since then, and he had announced to the village that today would mark the beginning of a new year. Everything depended on this date.

When it reached its farthest point south, its Winter House, the Sun reversed direction and moved back to the north, toward its Summer House. He knew that would happen today, that this would be the shortest day of the whole year. But he needed a clear sky to make his prayers at the Sun Shrine.

All through this night the men of the village had prayed and smoked sacred tobacco in the two ceremonial underground rooms, the *kivas*. They asked the Creator for a good year for their crops and for blessings of rain, health, and long life.

In the dark the Sun Watcher had left them and gone up to the cliff. He alone marked the dawn at this shrine.

The snow stopped falling. The pale sandstone had turned a rich butterscotch color as it absorbed the melting snow. Black streaks of natural desert varnish and orange and green patches of lichen patterned the cliff. The rising Sun broke the horizon and burned through the storm clouds, brightening the cold gray sky. Great Horned Owl called, *"Whoo, whooo, whoo-whooooooo."*

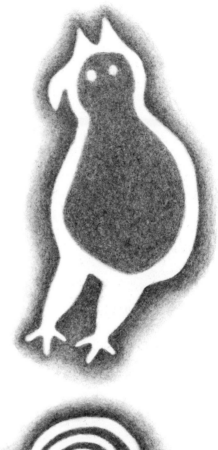

5

Standing up, the old man wrapped himself in his turkey-feather blanket. His sandals woven from yucca made soft prints in the wet sand between the sharp-angled boulders. He watched as a line of sunlight came through a narrow crack between two boulders and moved down the cliff. The pale yellow beam came closer and closer to a spiral carved on the rock many years before by another Sun Watcher to record the events of this special day.

As the Sun rose higher, the beam cut the very center of the spiral. The Sun Watcher sang his chants; he placed a prayer feather in the bottom of the crack between the boulders. The time had come.

The Sun Watcher returned to the village. On our calendar it was A.D. December 21, 1100. The winter solstice, the shortest day and longest night of the year, would be that very day. Each family in the Village of Blue Stone left its home in the soft darkness, walked past the turkeys clucking in their pens, and stood together at the east edge of the village to pray to the Sun as it rose on this day. In the cold morning air their voices rang out clearly over the canyon. The boom of their hide-covered drums echoed back to them from the far cliff.

The people pushed into the earth dozens of willow wands decorated with feathers—turkey, eagle, and hawk—and then sprinkled them with sacred cornmeal. Each man and woman, each boy and girl, had prayer sticks to offer—for their ancestors, for every living animal and plant, for the clouds, for all the unborn people still to come. The sunlight streamed through the prayer sticks plunged into the earth at the edge of the cliff, and the downy feathers twirled on their cotton strings in the winter wind. Now the days would grow longer.

The people of the village walked back to their homes, eager to feast on meat and corn that the women had prepared.

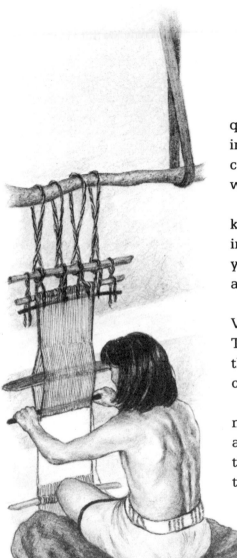

Winter was long and quiet. The men spent most of their time in the kivas, making and repairing tools, carving turquoise, and weaving. They hung their looms from the kiva roof, weaving sashes and dance kilts and blankets from cotton. They traded carved turquoise for cotton with people who lived farther south, where it was warm enough for cotton to grow.

After dark on these long winter nights, the people gathered in the kivas, the warmest and most comfortable places in the village, with indoor fireplaces and roof holes for the smoke to escape through. The year had spun around to the time for storytelling. Even the women and children were allowed in the kivas for stories.

The two kivas were crowded. Twenty-five people lived in the Village of Blue Stone. They belonged to six families and two clans. The Sun Watcher and the families of his sisters were all members of the Butterfly Clan. The Blue Corn Clan was in charge of the summer corn dance.

Clans were more important than family. Each boy or girl was a member of his or her mother's clan. The women owned all the houses and land. Their husbands lived with them but had more authority over their sisters' children, their nieces and nephews, than they did over their own children, who were members of their mother's clan and looked to their uncles for guidance. Clans did not control the kivas, however; a boy joined a kiva under the sponsorship of a "ceremonial father" who was not a member of his clan.

In the kivas the old men waited for everyone to gather and be still. Then they began. The Sun Watcher, whose name was Badger Claws, told the story of how The People had come through the four worlds. First the Yellow World, where the Creator had fashioned the First People. Then the Blue World, the Second World, where some of The People escaped when the First World was destroyed.

But again The People were led astray, and only the good people survived to emerge into the Third World, the Red World. Once more their evil ways brought on their destruction, and only The People with good hearts reached this present Fourth World, a Yellow-White World lit with the warmth of Father Sun.

Crane Flying, a Blue Corn elder, told the stories of the migrations that Blue Corn People completed once they reached this world. Each clan found its own way, as the Medicine Men prophesied, until Blue Corn People and Butterfly People settled here in the Village of Blue Stone. Other clans settled in other villages. Every winter, on special nights, the elders told these stories.

A grandmother, Corn Tassel Woman, the female leader of the

9

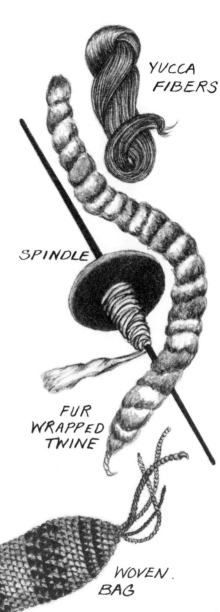

YUCCA FIBERS

SPINDLE

FUR WRAPPED TWINE

WOVEN BAG

Butterfly Clan, told the story about the Ant People, who taught The People how to be industrious. She told of Rabbit and Bighorn Sheep and Deer. Her brother, Badger Claws, told of powerful Bear and Mountain Lion, Badger and Snake, and of Horned Lizard, whose gift to The People was long life. And all the storytellers took turns with stories about Coyote—funny, greedy, foolish, wise, cruel, magical, unpredictable—Coyote the trickster.

Children heard the stories and listened with awe. Or they laughed and laughed at Coyote. But sometimes they heard a story they knew was for them. If they had done something wrong, an elder would tell a story that reminded them of the right way to live.

The elder wouldn't name the child or speak of his or her mistake. But when misbehaving children heard some story about the Warrior Twins, the great heroes of The People, or a story about Coyote or Rabbit, they would know the story was for them. When they passed the place where the story took place, they would hear the story in their memory and know what they needed to do to live right, to live like one of The People.

10

Two moons after the Sun began its journey back to its Summer House, the village celebrated the Bean Ceremony. Delicate green bundles of bean plants that the men had carefully sprouted in the warm kivas were given to each family on a frosty morning. This encouraged the coming of spring. Not long after, the men would begin clearing their fields. Warm weather would come and planting time would soon follow. The year was moving through its cycle of seasons and work and ceremonies.

In April, Rainy Dawn, the husband of the Sun Watcher's niece, went into the dark storage chamber behind the room where he and his family slept. Now was the time to plant his first crop. Here stood a huge pottery jar filled with seed corn and covered with a stone slab to keep the kernels from insects and mice. It was a white pot with black designs swirling around it in lines and steps and angles. Its surface was cold and smooth. Other jars held red and white corn, but this one held blue corn, the purplish blue kernels with the best flavor of all, sweet and nutty.

As he emptied the seeds into a woven twine bag to carry to the fields, he slipped on the smooth stone floor and bumped the great pottery jar. The pot was empty enough to jostle against the rock wall, and when he stopped it from wobbling, he found that it had cracked. Angry with himself for being careless, he called to his wife, Frog Woman.

Sometimes she repaired such a crack with a rawhide strip stretched tight around the pot to keep it from cracking further. But this time Frog Woman decided to make a new pot.

12

The next morning she left the village and hiked across two canyons to the place where she dug her clay. This was hard work. She had to reach deep into a small cave and knock off pieces of raw clay with a sharp stick. The clay was so rich that it looked like gray chocolate. When she had filled a basket with all she could carry, she sprinkled a cornmeal offering for Old Clay Woman, thanking her for her gift.

Frog Woman carried the clay home, bent beneath her load. She had to carry the thirty pounds of clay two miles, crossing one canyon, then another. Down and up, down and up again. Salty sweat ran into her eyes. She walked slowly, but she was strong and had no need to rest until she reached the Village of Blue Stone.

Frog Woman cleaned her clay in an old pot. She soaked it for three days, draining off the muddy water and straining out the sticks and stones, putting in fresh water every morning. Then she dried the clean clay, ground it on her grinding stone, and wet it to just the right consistency. She mixed in a fine powder ground from broken pieces of pottery called *potsherds*, to keep the rich clay from drying too fast and cracking.

13

With the old pottery pieces mixed into the new clay, many generations of potters and pottery became part of each new jar. It was a little like when Old Clay Woman first taught The People how to make pottery. She gave every woman in the First Village a piece of clay to work with. Maybe some of that clay was reused and reused and reused until now it was in this pot.

Finally Frog Woman was ready to build her pot, one hand-rolled coil at a time.

With a vessel this big, she had to build in stages over several days, adding a few coils and then smoothing them, then repeating her steps. While the woman made her big jar, her daughter, Dragonfly, took some clay and worked on a small pot, trying to make it as smooth and graceful as her mother's.

The mother worked until her pot was almost two feet high. Now she could let it dry. After it dried, she still had to sand it smooth with a lump of rough sandstone, coat the surface with white clay, polish it with a smooth pebble, and paint on her designs. Her daughter followed her movements. Only after Dragonfly had done each step once on her own did the mother correct her.

Frog Woman decided to do something special with the design of this pot, something she had seen only once before. In the bold bands of black designs, she left a space on each side of the pot, and in this space she painted a butterfly—she belonged to the Butterfly Clan. Dragonfly chose a familiar black-banded design that meant clouds, to help bring rain to the corn. They used black paint made from the boiled leaves of beeplant. They painted with yucca-leaf brushes, carefully shaping their lines to the form of each pot.

When they finished painting their designs, they gathered pieces of dead juniper from the mesa. At the edge of the village they built a fire and baked their pots, firing them hard. Many other times the pottery broke in the fire, and all their work was wasted. But this time both the huge pot and the smaller one came out perfect. The big pot rang like a bell when Dragonfly carefully rapped its rim with her knuckle.

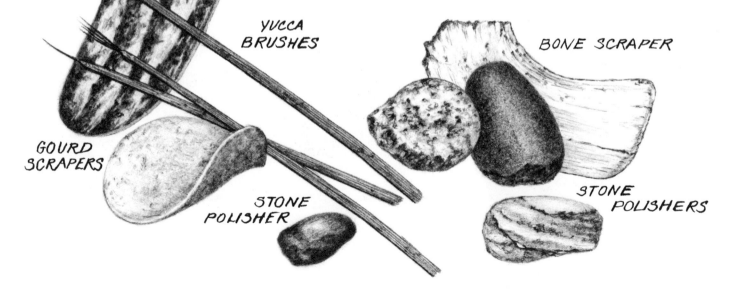

GOURD SCRAPERS

YUCCA BRUSHES

STONE POLISHER

BONE SCRAPER

STONE POLISHERS

Dragonfly's father was up on the mesa working his fields with her younger brother, Turquoise Boy. Now they were planting the early corn, then in May, squash and beans. In June all the men planted the main corn crop, hoping that they had missed the worst of the spring winds—and praying for the coming of summer rains.

Rainy Dawn had carved his digging stick from greasewood, a shrub that always grows near water. The tool felt cool and smooth in his hands at first, but as he worked, it became sweaty and stuck to his fingers. He pushed it into the ground about wrist deep, carefully placing twelve to fifteen kernels of corn in the bottom of the hole. He knelt to dig only about every ten feet, so that each plant would not have to compete with the others for water.

Turquoise Boy wove small windbreaks from grass and twigs or propped up slabs of sandstone to shelter the growing corn from the hot glare of the Sun. He set traps for rabbits, dug out weeds, and packed the dirt around the plants with his feet to make it more difficult for worms trying to burrow into the roots.

17

The young men ran races along the edges of the fields, offering their speed to encourage the plants to grow rapidly. They built shrines by the green corn and stood in the rows and prayed for rain clouds to come and shower their fields. As the corn ripened, farmers even slept by the fields so that they could be there to chase away the ravens and rabbits that came to nibble on the plants.

The growing corn was the center of the villagers' lives through the summer. But many other things took time as well. As they did all year, the women ground corn in early morning and in the evening. They talked and sang corn-grinding songs while they worked. Sweet grain smells filled the east plaza where the grinding bins stood in a row. The movement of the women's stone *manos* back and forth across the *metate* troughs was one of the most beautiful rhythms of the village.

During the day the women searched for wild food plants. They filled their baskets with tiny golden seeds knocked from dry fruits with a stick. They gathered greens and dug thick roots from the sandy soil. Men snared small animals in the fields—gophers and rabbits, prairie dogs and ground squirrels. All these foods went into the cook pot. Some animals were roasted on a spit over hot coals. Other meats and plants were dried and pounded for storage.

The people began to prepare for the summer dances. In summer they danced here in the Village of Blue Stone, asking the Cloud People for rain. The dances brought clouds from the six directions, from the east, south, west, and north, from the zenith, the sky, and from the nadir, the earth. And the clouds brought rain.

To make sure the people would be able to send their prayers to the sky when the time came, the men captured eagles and hawks and brought them back to the village. Eagles were messengers to the Cloud People, and their feathers gave power to prayer sticks.

Young men made the very best eagle catchers. They were agile enough to climb up the cliffs or lower themselves down braided yucca ropes into the aeries where eagles nested high on rock faces or in the crooks of tall cottonwood trees. The eagle catchers captured the young birds before they could fly. They had to carry sticks to keep away the parent eagles that swooped down with their talons outstretched, defending their eaglets. The young men had to be brave.

This summer the eagle catchers did well. They caught six hawks and five young golden eagles. The Hunting Priest's son, Blue Spruce, captured three eaglets from a single nest built on a narrow ledge below Twin Rocks. The men carefully wrapped the eagles and took them back to the village, tying each of them by one leg with a soft cotton string to a stake on the roofs of the houses. They caught mice, kangaroo rats, and grasshoppers to feed them, and slowly the eaglets grew. At sunrise and at sunset, when they flapped their wings, their silhouettes gave the whole village an eerie feeling, a feeling of power, of connection with the sky.

21

As the eagles grew during the next few months, so did the village. During this summer, three babies were born. One died with her mother during birth. Another was a sickly boy, but he lived. The third was a strong boy born to the Hunting Priest's youngest aunt, Reed Woman, into the Blue Corn Clan. When he was born, the first gift he received was from his godmother—a perfect ear of white corn: a Corn Mother to represent his spiritual mother and to remind him of all his ties to the Earth and to Mother Corn, to life.

On the morning of the baby's fourth day of life, the leader of the Medicine Society came to the house of the newborn boy. The Medicine Man's wife washed the baby in purifying yucca-root suds and washed the mother's hair, as well. Then the Medicine Man took the baby out to the east edge of the mesa and presented him to rising Father Sun, officially giving him the name his parents had chosen.

This boy was called Blue Feather, to remind him that though he was a member of his mother's Blue Corn Clan, he had some of his father's power, too. His father, Sun Journeying, was from the clan named for an animal of the skies—Butterfly, an animal that could fly like the feathered birds.

Blue Feather, like all the babies of the village, spent much of his first year bound in a cradleboard. He was wrapped in fine cotton and rabbit fur blankets woven by his father in the kiva, with soft juniper bark under him. He was taken out only for washing and to change the absorbent juniper bark—his "diapers."

Reed Woman nursed him, and his parents and grandparents sang to him, but he was in his cradleboard most of the time. During this time the cradleboard permanently flattened the back of his head, so he would look like all the other villagers. Unbound after a year, he began to explore the village around him.

While Blue Feather was in his cradleboard during his first summer, his uncle, Crane Flying, began the preparations for the Corn Dance. He was the male Blue Corn Clan leader. All the Blue Corn People would dance, while the Butterfly People watched. It was just as important to watch as to dance, for everyone's good thoughts would bring the rain.

The dancers practiced for many long hours in the kiva. Blue Feather's cousin, Buffalo Man, the Hunting Priest, wrote a new song for the ceremony. It told the story of how The People came to this world and it invited the Cloud People to hear their prayers and to come to their fields. The elders taught the dancers the proper steps. Finally two men went north to the mountains for sacred spruce. They walked and climbed until they found the big trees growing by the sacred spring. From Spruce, the tree that is a magnet for rain clouds, they cut fragrant boughs to bring back for the dancers to wear.

On the dance day the clan leaders made a path of cornmeal from the kiva entrances to the plaza, and the dancers came out into the sunlight, moving to the rhythm of songs and drums.

All of the women and men carried branches of sacred spruce as they swayed from side to side. All of their motions and thoughts were aimed at the Cloud People, to bring rain to the corn. They danced to the east, south, west, and north; then they raised up their prayers to the heavens and returned below to the kiva to rest before coming out again to dance.

They danced round after round during the day. And when they were finished, the people took the spruce boughs, now made even more powerful by the dance, and stood them in their fields. The dancers returned home. Mothers and fathers, wives and husbands made purifying yucca suds and washed each other's hair and the hair of their children who had danced, marking the return to everyday life.

After the dance the time had come to send the hawks and eagles home to the sky. The clan leaders went onto the roofs of the houses and, with prayers, gently smothered the great birds. The men thanked the spirit of Eagle and Hawk for the gift of their feathers to be used in the people's prayer sticks. The plucked birds were buried in the sacred eagle and hawk burying ground at the edge of the village with offerings of cornmeal and prayer feathers.

And the clouds came and gently soaked the fields of corn, the terraces of beans, and the plots of squash. Rain soaked into the ground, nourishing the young plants, ensuring good life for the people of the Village of Blue Stone.

25

Not long after the Corn Dance, a happy day came to the village. The Trader arrived from the south, bringing parrot feathers for dance costumes and shells from the far ocean. Everyone welcomed him and prepared a feast, asking him many questions about the larger villages he had visited. He came from the Canyon of Great Houses, the center of The People's religion. He was a priest as well as a trader.

In return the villagers traded turquoise. The village had several master carvers who worked the blue stone into whatever shapes could be imagined. They created animals, used to make offerings in hunting season or to ask for help from a powerful brother or sister like Bear or Mountain Lion. They inlaid bits of turquoise into bone hide-scrapers and into carved shell jewelry, into cottonwood-backed earrings with patterns of turquoise and black jet and white shell. They covered ceremonial bowls and cylinders with inlays the color of the sky. And they cut and drilled turquoise beads with a hand-pumped wooden drill, grinding them round by rolling them against a piece of sandstone, stringing them by the hundreds in necklaces.

If they could find clays and minerals and stone for carving near enough to their homes, villagers gathered their own supplies. Beyond that, they relied on trade. The Village of Blue Stone traded for their turquoise with other villages that were closer to the mines, villages far to the east, beyond the mountains.

Each year, the Trader from the south saved some of his most beautiful parrot feathers for the Village of Blue Stone. He knew he would have to drive a hard bargain for the finest work in the village. Sometimes he even brought a live scarlet macaw, carried in a cage on the backs of traders all the way up from what is now called Mexico.

The squawks of these parrots always made the Trader laugh as he walked along the road northward from the Canyon of Great Houses, stopping to make his prayers and offerings at the shrines and sacred springs along the way. The birds always seemed so wonderfully out of place in the dry plateau, too dry even for piñon and juniper trees. They were truly a special gift.

In July and August dawn came to the village clear and hot. Canyon Wren's call cut through the still air like the notes from a wooden flute. But later each morning the Cloud People began to stir. By midafternoon towering white thunderheads built up over the mountains and sailed out over the cornfields of the village. Thunder cracked the heavy, humid air. Lightning bolts reached down from the gray sky to shatter and burn piñon and juniper trees along ridgetops. And rain came to the crops.

By sunset the clouds had passed through and disappeared. A crescent moon hung in a clear lavender sky, and the air smelled clean and sharp. The corn grew and ripened, and The People gave thanks.

Autumn came—with long bright days after the thunderstorm season. Rabbitbrush blossomed yellow along the white sandstone rim of the canyon. Pinyon Jay *craaaked* through the forest, harvesting the ripe nuts from the piñon pines. When the women went down to the spring to fill their water jars, they saw golden leaves of cottonwood trees and brilliant blue sky reflected in the cold pools.

The first frost ended the growing season for the corn. The plants turned yellow-gold in the autumn sun, and in October the men went out to gather the ears. It was a good harvest. They carried bundle after bundle back to the village, where the women and children sat shucking the ears. They were almost lost in the piles of red, white, blue, and speckled corn and dry, papery husks. After sorting the corn by color, each family dried it on the rooftops before storing it inside. They bundled the husks to use for torches in the kivas.

A year like this, with a surplus of corn, was a gift from the Cloud People. With gratitude the villagers filled their storage rooms to the roofs. This corn could last them through a full year or two of drought, even if the crops and wild plants failed them completely.

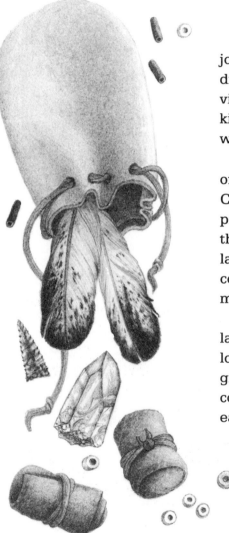

It was time to give thanks. After the harvest each year, the people danced in the Great Kiva at Big River Village, a day's journey south. Everyone but the oldest elders and the youngest children prepared to go. The women ground corn to take to the larger village. The men prepared their medicine bundles and prayed in the kivas that all would go well with the journey and the dance. They waited for the signal from Big River Village, telling them it was time.

When the runner appeared on the road from the south, the people of the Village of Blue Stone were ready. The women chose perfect Corn Mothers from the harvest for the dancers to hold. The men tied prayer feathers around these ears, and each person carried one. Along the way people from other villages joined them. When they neared the large village, dozens of people were arriving from the surrounding country. Children who were making their first trip had never seen so many people in one place.

Nor had they seen such a large village, and certainly not such a large building as the Great Kiva, forty-eight feet across—almost as long as the whole Village of Blue Stone. It stood in the plaza aboveground, and the Kiva Chiefs, standing quietly, wearing embroidered cotton kilts, their faces and bodies painted with white clay, guarded each of its entrances.

30

The people from the Village of Blue Stone stayed with their clan relatives and prepared for the dance the next day. The women started cooking immediately, making white corn cakes and paper-thin *piki* bread from blue cornmeal for the dancers to eat. The men went to the kivas to fast and pray all night.

The next day everyone prepared for the Harvest Dance. Priests painted the faces of the dancers and blessed them with cornmeal. Lines of dancers gathered in the smaller kivas and then danced through the plaza into the Great Kiva. Going from bright sunlight into the dusky, smoky interior of the sacred building felt like entering the underworld. Row upon row of dancers passed by each other, each dancing in a circle and then returning to their smaller kiva. The chanting and drumming echoed in the large chamber like the heartbeat of the Earth.

Three rounds of dancing completed the thanksgiving. That evening the Big River Village families and their visitors feasted on the new corn. They slept contentedly, knowing they had done the proper thing for the Cloud People, thanking them for this good harvest.

The visitors stayed for several days, talking and feasting with their clans. Then, one morning, when they awoke to a bright new dawn, the people of the Village of Blue Stone left for home.

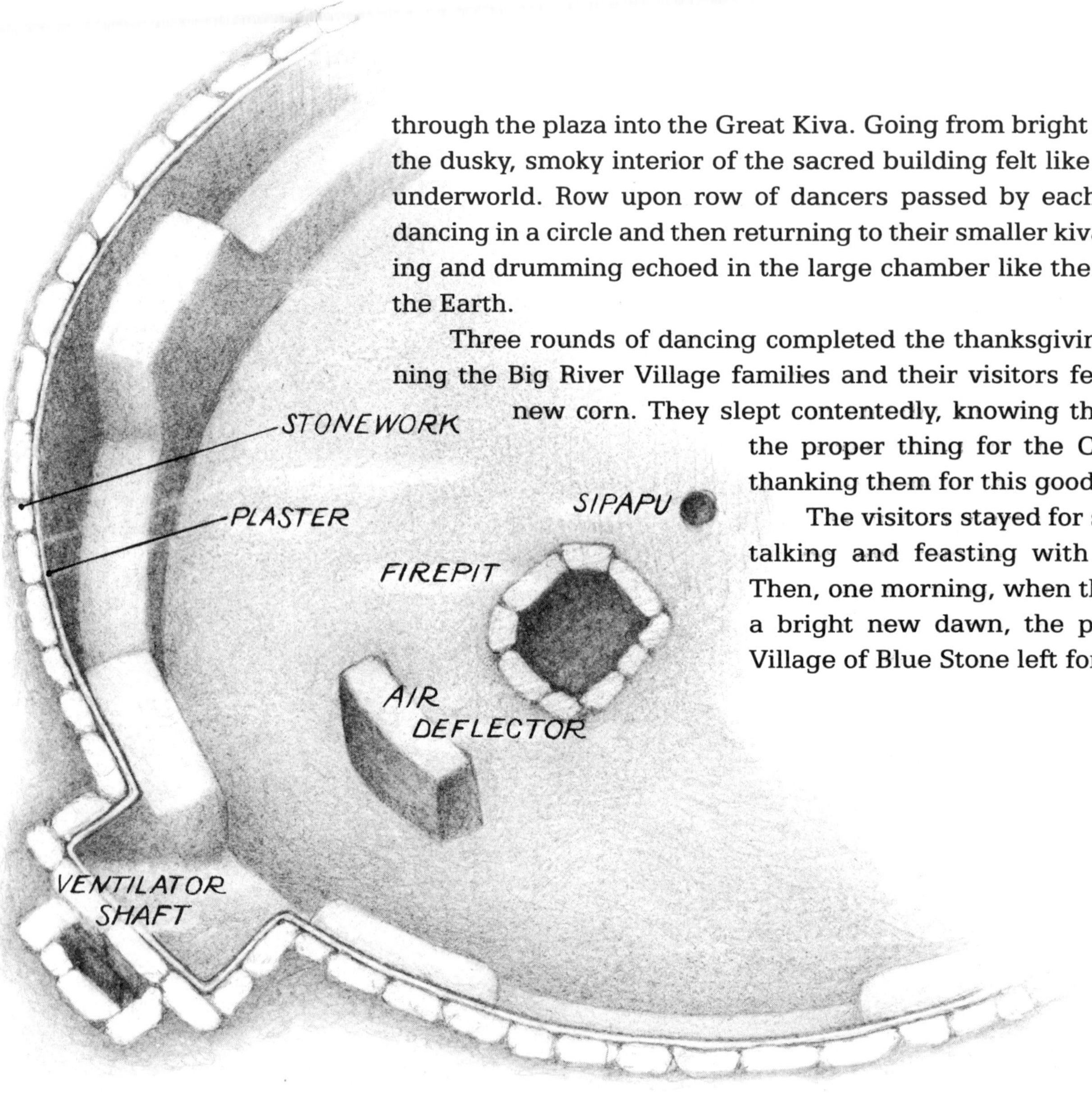

STONEWORK

PLASTER

SIPAPU

FIREPIT

AIR DEFLECTOR

VENTILATOR SHAFT

The villagers split up on the way back, to take advantage of being out in new country. Several women and their children stopped to gather piñon nuts. Young boys climbed to the tops of the little pine trees to shake the branches and rain nuts down in a clatter from the open cones. The mothers and daughters filled basket after basket with nuts. Later they would have to shell them to reach the delicately flavored seeds.

One of the men left the road to take a higher ridge homeward. He moved slowly, for he hoped to find mule deer moving down from the mountains to the oak-brush country where deer spend their winters.

The hunter, Sun Journeying, was Blue Feather's father. His *fetish* was a turquoise mountain lion, hunter of deer. He fingered the carved stone lion in his medicine bag, asking Deer to help The People live through the winter. He moved slowly, bow ready to be drawn. He did his best to think like a deer, to move like a deer, to *be* a deer.

Luck was with him.

Sun Journeying found the tracks of a small band of young bucks. He squatted over their trail; he knew that they were moving up a small canyon, that they had passed here within the hour, and that they would bed down for most of the day in the shade of the cliffrose and

33

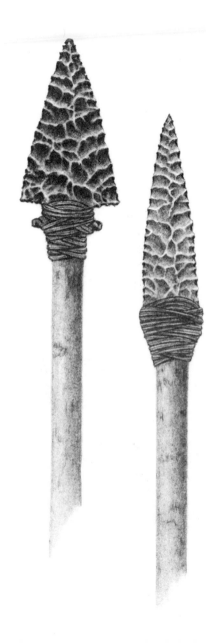

serviceberry thickets. He circled above them, downwind, and moved silently back down the canyon. When Sun Journeying saw them, he was very close. They still did not see him.

Blue Feather's father raised his bow. He asked respectfully for Deer's permission for him to take its life to give food to all of his family. He silently sang his hunting song while he let the arrow fly. The chipped flint head struck true. The herd bolted over the hill, but the deer he had wounded could not run. It walked haltingly only a few yards and disappeared into the brush. He followed it, and when he saw it lie down, he ran to the dying buck.

The man put his mouth up to the muzzle of the deer. Singing to it softly, he breathed in the last of the deer's sweet breaths, the Breath of Life. Sun Journeying made a cornmeal blessing, thanking the deer for its sacrifice, and laid its head toward the east, toward the Sun. When he cleaned it, he cut off a small piece of flesh to leave for Mother Earth. Then he shouldered the soft-furred animal and headed home to the Village of Blue Stone, singing all the while.

The potter's daughter, Dragonfly, had been watching Blue Spruce, the son of the Hunting Priest. He was a shy young man, but she admired him because he was smart and careful and thoughtful in what he said. During the Harvest Dance, she slipped into his hands two corn cakes wrapped in fresh white corn husks and tied together. His heart began racing, and he blushed when he felt them in his palm. He knew this meant she wanted him as her husband.

He had been watching her, too. She was strong, and already she could make pots nearly as fine as her mother's. And so their courtship began. Blue Spruce came to Dragonfly while she ground corn, flattering her and making her laugh. The other women teased him hard, but he stayed with her.

They sat together on the terrace of the village. Dragonfly combed Blue Spruce's hair with bundles of long ponderosa pine needles. He wove a special bag for her in the kiva. Their parents agreed to the match. No one in their clans opposed it. The families began to prepare the formal exchanges of corn and weaving.

The girl's family was responsible for feeding the whole village during the wedding ceremony; all the women helped Dragonfly to grind corn and make piki. The bride ground and ground, and when enough cornmeal was piled high in baskets, the wedding ceremony could take place.

The men in Blue Spruce's family meanwhile had helped him to weave wedding clothes from fine cotton for his bride—two blankets and a sash.

On the wedding day both mothers together washed the hair of the bride and groom. Then the bride's mother did up her daughter's hair in the married woman's style, hanging down in loops instead of tightly done up in the whorls of an unmarried girl. After the hair washing, Dragonfly wore the new blankets and sash as the villagers

36

walked with her in a procession from Blue Spruce's home at one end of the pueblo to the girl's home at the other end, where they would live until they built a room of their own.

The wedding dominated the life of the Village of Blue Stone for most of November. Almost everyone did something for the couple's families, and all shared in the feast. The new young bride and her husband took care to remember just who helped the most. Over the years they would be careful to repay these favors, showing their gratitude in the way of The People.

While the villagers were busy with the wedding, winter came to their canyon. Cottonwood leaves dried. Winds rattled them until they broke loose and twirled to the ground in drifts. The sunlight remained warm, but the air grew cooler and cooler. The sky turned a deeper and deeper blue as the angle of the Sun dropped lower.

As the days grew colder, the people spent much of their time working to stay warm. Each day as they did their tasks, they moved with the Sun from the east plaza, where the stone walls caught the first light, to the west plaza, where the last rays hit in afternoon. They spent more time indoors, more time by the fires, more time gathering firewood.

One day in late November Frog Woman was working over the cooking fire in her room—it was too windy to cook outside and certainly the wrong season to work on her pottery. A storm was blowing in from the west, and the air cut right through her rabbit-skin robe. She heard intent voices outside, dogs barking, and went out to see what was happening.

The runner from the Canyon of Great Houses had come, announcing the winter initiation. When girls and boys were old enough, about nine or ten, they made the three-day pilgrimage all the way south to this sacred place for the most important ceremony of their youths. As

38

they did every year, the clan leaders would make the journey south, even though this year the Village of Blue Stone had no children of initiation age.

While Frog Woman was out in the plaza watching the runner disappear into a kiva with the men, she heard a cry behind her.

The wind had whipped through the small door opening into her room and fanned her cooking fire into a blaze. The wooden beams of her room were in flames. Black smoke poured from her doorway. People gathered around. She ran in to save her blankets, especially her daughter Dragonfly's new wedding blankets. But the smoke was already too thick. Her father yelled at her, "Quick! Jam a sandstone slab over the doorway to block off the room." She did this and waited for the fire to die out.

Her father told her she must leave the room closed until morning or it would start burning again when she opened the door. So she and her family spent that night next door, in her mother's rooms. The next morning they were able to open the burned room, pour water on the beams to stop their smoldering, and begin to sweep out the soot with brooms of twigs. Two beams had collapsed at the rear of the room and would have to be replaced. The others were charred but still strong. Her blankets and skins—and Dragonfly's, too—were all ruined.

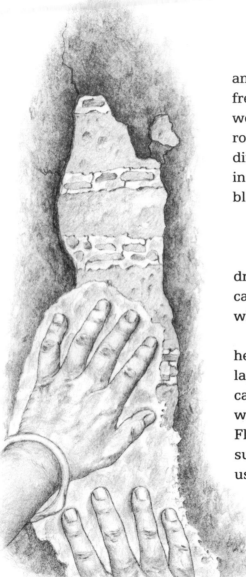

All the people helped to fix the room, the men cutting new beams and the women replastering the walls. It was so cold the plaster kept freezing, but they were able at least to chink the biggest cracks. They would finish the job in summer, when they would also build a separate room for Dragonfly and Blue Spruce. Clan relatives gave enough bedding to keep the family warm. Within only two weeks they were back in their own room, which was almost as good as ever except for the blackened roof.

The wife of Crane Flying was sick. Her life was slipping away. Hummingbird Flower had lived long and raised many children and grandchildren. Each member of her family and her clan came and sat with her, talked to her, asked her to live. She did not hear what they said.

In the night, when her husband and oldest daughter were with her, Hummingbird Flower stopped breathing. She was old for a villager; she had lived fifty years. Her clan women, the Butterfly women, came the next morning, bathing her a last time in yucca suds and wrapping her in her best cotton blanket. At the same time Crane Flying and their sons dug a grave for her in the soft mounds that surrounded the western edge of the village, mounds of earth and refuse from all the years people had lived here. The people did not think of it as a dumping ground, but rather as a sacred place, where all things rejoined Mother Earth, from fireplace ashes, broken pottery, and corn cobs to the bodies of their loved ones.

The men carried Hummingbird Flower's body to the grave. All of her relatives prayed for her safe passage and for her easy return to them as a Cloud Person. The woman had been a potter, so they buried her with two of her best pots and her pottery-making tools—her scrapers made from squash rind, her polishing stones, her paints and yucca brushes. They dusted all of these with sacred cornmeal, and then they covered the grave.

That night a snowstorm came and blanketed the village, the woodland, and the grave. The next day was clear, and the snow quickly melted into the sandy earth. When the villagers looked out over the ash mounds, they couldn't tell where the new grave had been dug. Already Hummingbird Flower had journeyed back to her Mother, the Earth.

More storms came; more snow fell. Then, after each storm, the Sun would come out again, and the people would sit out in the plazas of the village, working. Ravens and magpies hopped up to the edge of the pueblo, trying to steal tidbits of food. Children and dogs chased them away.

It was winter. The days grew shorter and shorter. Badger Claws, the Sun Watcher, began to spend his mornings in the Sun Shrine room. He knew the solstice was approaching.

He also knew he was getting old. His teeth were almost completely ground away from eating corn always mixed with a little sand from the grinding stones. His joints hurt on these cold winter days. He would be able to announce the time for the winter solstice for only a few more years. He needed to teach a younger man the ways of sun watching.

And so for the past year he had watched the men and thought about which one would be best to choose to honor his Father, the Sun.

He had decided. His oldest sister's son, Black Falling Snow, who had lived a good life, who had raised his children well, and who was one of the storytellers, was his choice. He needed a man, not a boy, a man who was wise in the ways of living but not so old that he would die soon after Badger Claws died.

42

He smoked with his nephew, sitting on the floor of their kiva. He began to tell him the stories of the Sun. They went to the shrine room and laid offerings of cornmeal and prayer feathers in the wall niches. He taught the younger man his songs and his prayers so that his apprentice could sing the Sun along to its Winter House and know the right song to sing the Sun back again to the summer—to sing warmth to the village, to sing up the springtime.

Black Falling Snow took this honor seriously and studied hard. He sang the songs over and over. He said the prayers while he worked on other things. Together the two men announced that the time was soon. They picked the day, the shortest day of the year.

And the night before the day came that would complete another year in the village, two Sun Watchers went up on the cliff to fast in the cold starry night, leaving the other men to pray in the kiva. Together they waited for dawn to come. They were ready when the yellow Sun rose. It cast its dagger of sunlight on the cliff wall. The two men watched as the dagger cut the spiral in two, marking the first day of another good year for the Village of Blue Stone.

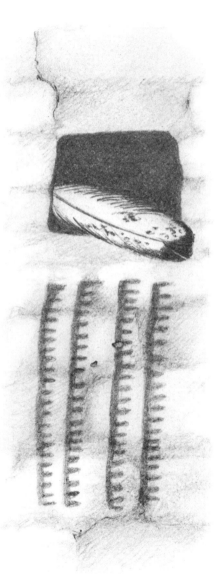

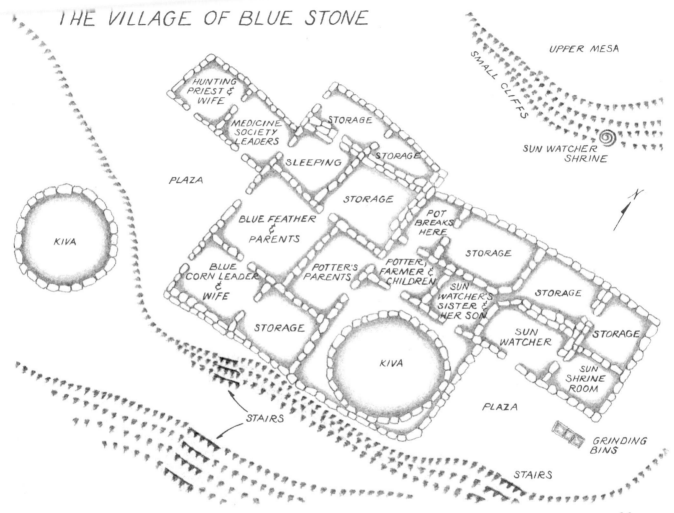

THE VILLAGE OF BLUE STONE

UPPER MESA

SMALL CLIFFS

SUN WATCHER SHRINE

HUNTING PRIEST & WIFE

MEDICINE SOCIETY LEADERS

STORAGE

STORAGE

SLEEPING

STORAGE

PLAZA

STORAGE

KIVA

BLUE FEATHER & PARENTS

POT BREAKS HERE

STORAGE

BLUE CORN LEADER & WIFE

POTTER'S PARENTS

POTTER, FARMER & CHILDREN

SUN WATCHER'S SISTER & HER SON

STORAGE

STORAGE

STORAGE

KIVA

SUN WATCHER

STAIRS

SUN SHRINE ROOM

PLAZA

GRINDING BINS

STAIRS

44

RELATIONSHIPS OF MAIN CHARACTERS

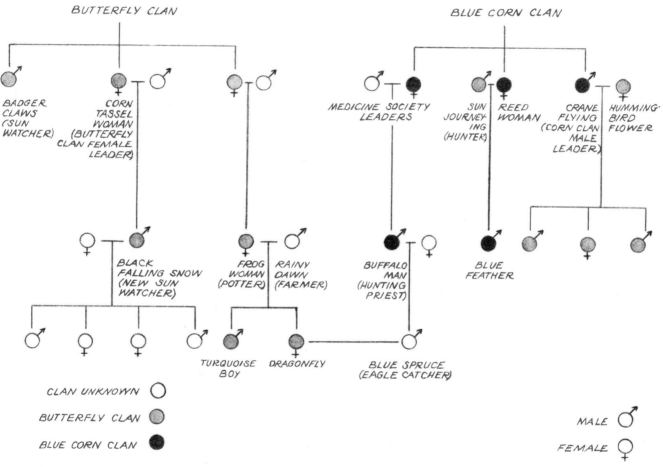

CLAN UNKNOWN ◯

BUTTERFLY CLAN ◍

BLUE CORN CLAN ●

MALE ♂

FEMALE ♀

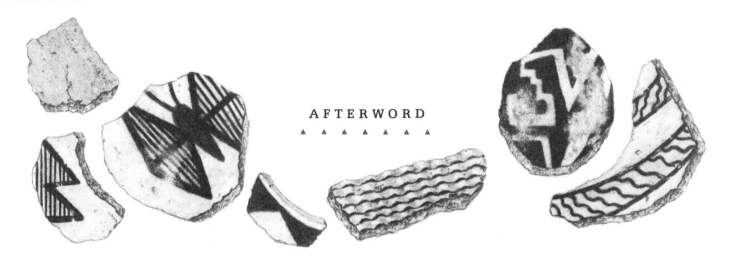

The two archaeologists were just beginning their survey of Ruin N-J300, also known by the name the Wetherill brothers had given it in 1892, Turquoise House. The man and woman were working on a contract with the San Juan County Historical Society, documenting all the outlying villages north of the San Juan River in New Mexico that showed connections with the Chaco culture—the first great flowering of Anasazi civilization.

"Mummy Lake Gray. Mancos Black-on-white. Mesa Verde Corrugated. Cibola Black-on-white—means there's some tradeware."

The archaeologists moved through the ruin, picking up pieces of broken pottery. They knew their pottery types so well that it took only a glance to identify them. Since they knew when each pottery type was made, they could date the ruin by its pottery: late eleventh or early twelfth century.

"Socorro Black-on-white, more tradeware. McElmo Black-on-white. Exuberant Corrugated."

Then the woman noticed a sherd unlike any of the others.

"Hey, Robert, look at this." Mary held out her hand, cradling a sherd with black-on-white paint. It looked like a butterfly nestling in her palm, for one was elegantly painted on the pottery piece, flying across the side of a long-broken jar. Neither archaeologist had ever seen anything like it. Whoever made that pot must have been very special.

The two put the unusual butterfly pot-sherd in a sample sack and gave it a tag number that indicated its location. Later they would analyze the content of its clay, paint, and temper, and see if they could tell where it had been made.

They looked long and hard among the fallen walls and between the shrubs growing in the old pueblo. Most of the potsherds, as well as the turquoise that had given the ruin its name, had been taken away over the years by visitors to the ruin, beginning with the Wetherill brothers. Though the Wetherills weren't trained as archaeologists (hardly anyone was in the 1800s), the brothers did sell their collections to museums, where the bracelets, baskets, and pottery they collected still can be seen.

Robert and Mary had a much more diffi-cult job. So many artifacts were missing.

The two archaeologists had been working all morning. They walked up to the mesa top, took their lunches from the pickup truck, and sat down in the shade of a juniper on the rim of the cliff. Robert looked out over the ruin. The walls of carefully shaped stone still stood four feet high, although the log ceilings had fallen in. Two doorways cut through one wall. A badger and a colony of ground squirrels had burrowed into the soil between the tumbled stones of the two kivas. A barely noticeable prehistoric road led south toward Aztec Ruins and still farther—sixty miles—to Chaco Canyon, center of the region's Anasazi culture.

Robert said, "I just can't understand why they left." Robert was an Acoma Pueblo Indian himself, and so his thoughts on the abandoned pueblos were more than just scientific questions: The Anasazi were his ancestors.

His partner, Mary, looked at the lush little canyon below, its cream-colored sandstone walls cut in winding curves by flash floods. Cottonwoods grew at its seeping spring, and the satisfying view out to the horizon reached all the way to the far purple haze of the Rocky Mountains.

The two knew that the Anasazi used a small village like this one for only about fifty years. When the villagers left, usually they moved just over the next hill, close by, probably to take advantage of new farming and firewood resources, or to take advantage of land made attractive by increased rainfall in some years.

But that didn't explain why such vast regions were abandoned. True, this was a dry, dry place for large populations and complex regional cultures. Chaco Canyon and Mesa Verde and the whole San Juan River country were all completely emptied by 1300. The weather had become more unpredictable. The people cut too many trees for firewood and roof beams; without trees to protect the soil against flooding, fields eroded away. Regional systems of government may have fallen apart when a drought or political crisis or some other problem came along. But the people always built another great complex of villages somewhere else. Eventually they moved to today's pueblos.

Archaeologists, even Pueblo archaeologists, cannot answer these questions simply. And to make their work even more challenging, they always hope to be a step ahead of pot hunters, people who dig in the ruins without concern for what they can learn, solely in search of artifacts to sell. Sometimes the vandals even bulldoze the old villages in search of pots and turquoise. When the archaeologists come a step behind the looters, their chances for careful excavation are gone, and a record of a past civilization is lost forever. It is impossible to guard every one of the thousands of ruins in the Southwest.

Mary and Robert hoped to add one more piece to the solution of the Anasazi puzzle. They decided to apply for research money to fund excavation of a test trench in the small ruin below them. They could only hope pot hunters would not reach the ruin before they could return.

▲▲▲▲▲▲▲▲▲▲▲▲▲▲▲▲▲▲▲▲▲▲▲▲▲▲

The crew member was down on his knees, working with a broom. Carefully, he brushed the dirt away from a skull. Ben was a student at the University of New Mexico in Albuquerque, hired by Mary and Robert to help in the summer's dig. The archaeologists' grant proposal had been funded; they were cutting through the ash mound of Turquoise

House and had been working here for a month.

Ben felt strange and respectful working with these bones, particularly because this skeleton might be one of Robert's direct ancestors. It seemed right to him that after excavation and study, the archaeologists planned to rebury all the bones here again in the ruin, where they belonged.

As Ben cleaned away the dirt to the left of the skull, he uncovered the rim of a pot. Slowly his work revealed two perfect pots that had been buried with this woman (he knew this was a woman because the excavation team's bone expert had looked at the shape of the bones and said so). And along with the pottery, there were pottery-making tools, polishing stones just like those he had seen Pueblo women using today, and small stone mortars with dried black paint still in them. This woman must have been a potter.

Ben straightened up to rest his back. He went over to watch the two chief archaeologists for a minute. Mary and Robert were taking wood samples from fallen beams, to be matched with the long chronology of tree rings back at the university.

Over many years of excavation, a calendar of tree rings had been made, so that scientists could date fragments of wood. They matched up the thin and thick rings of a new sample with the master calendar, and then could state just when a tree grew and when it was cut to be used for building.

"Easy with that beam!" Robert was saying. "It's so badly charred, I'm not sure whether we can get a date from it." He looked around the room. The other beams looked better. With luck, the cutting dates on the unburned ones would give them the year of the fire.

Robert was leaving the dig that afternoon. The following Saturday was Feast Day at Acoma Pueblo, celebrated on September 2 every year. His clan was dancing, so he needed to be at the pueblo to spend Thursday and Friday nights in the kiva, practicing for the Harvest Dance.

Although he had earned his doctor's degree in anthropology and now lived in Albuquerque, he felt as strongly as ever about participating in ceremonies back home. He always returned for feast days, and his parents were just as proud that he did so as

49

they were of his success at the university.

He gathered the tree-ring samples, along with the week's collection of turquoise beads, a beautiful turquoise-inlaid jet frog, and a copper bell traded all the way up from Mexico. These were too valuable to leave at the field camp, and he would take them to the university lab before driving on to Acoma Pueblo.

When he was ready, he talked with Mary about the plan for the next week; they agreed on the next steps the excavation should take. He wished Mary, Ben, and the rest of the crew good luck with the digging.

As Robert walked up the trail toward his pickup, a raven perched on the camper shell flew off with a squawk. Robert started the motor and drove off through the piñon and juniper trees. Only a quarter of a mile from the ruin, a coyote ran across the road, stopped, and turned to watch the archaeologist drive by.

The Acoma man knew about Coyote, the magical trickster, from the stories he heard his grandfather tell every winter. He stopped to look at the animal; he was sure Coyote was smiling at him. Robert smiled back and drove on, hoping to be home by sunset.

AUTHOR'S NOTE

▲ ▲ ▲ ▲ ▲ ▲ ▲ ▲ ▲ ▲

No one knows what life in an Anasazi village was like in every detail, but archaeologists have discovered many artifacts that tell us about Anasazi lives. And both archaeologists and modern Native Americans agree that the Pueblo people of today are the direct descendants of prehistoric Anasazi people.

In telling the story of the Village of Blue Stone, I have relied on technical books about Southwest archaeology. But much of the daily life I have described is the daily life of modern pueblos, particularly the Hopi pueblos in

Arizona and Zuni and Acoma pueblos in New Mexico.

Cliff dwellings came late in Anasazi history. Over most of the many centuries that the Anasazi lived in the Southwest, they lived in small mesa-top and open-valley pueblos like the village described in this story. The imaginary Village of Blue Stone is a small pueblo in the mesas north of the San Juan River, an outlying village of the great cultural center of Chaco Canyon (called the Canyon of Great Houses in my story), near Aztec Ruins National Monument (called Big River Village here). The story is set at the time when Chaco culture was most powerful: A.D. 1100.

If you can, visit an Anasazi ruin and try to imagine it a living place, full of people and emotion and drama.

▲▲▲▲▲▲▲▲▲▲▲▲▲▲▲▲▲▲▲▲▲▲▲▲▲▲▲

ANASAZI RUINS TO VISIT

Colorado
Anasazi Heritage Center, Dolores
Mesa Verde National Park, near Cortez
Ute Mountain Tribal Park, near Cortez

Utah
Edge of the Cedars State Historical Park, Blanding
Hovenweep National Monument, near Montezuma Creek
Canyonlands National Park, near Monticello

Arizona
Canyon de Chelly National Monument, near Chinle
Navajo National Monument, near Kayenta
Petrified Forest National Park, near Holbrook
Wupatki National Monument, near Flagstaff

New Mexico
Aztec Ruins National Monument, Aztec
Bandelier National Monument, near Los Alamos
Chaco Culture National Historic Park, near Farmington
El Morro National Monument, near Gallup

If you wish to help with an excavation of an important Anasazi site, contact Crow Canyon Center for Southwestern Archaeology, 23390 County Road K, Cortez, Colorado 81321.

Pueblo people still live in stone and adobe houses, make pottery, worship in kivas, farm cornfields, catch eagles for their feathers, and dance in thanksgiving for good harvests and for rain. Anasazi culture is not dead; it continues to give meaning to the lives of modern Pueblo Indian people.

For information on visiting modern pueblos and schedules of ceremonial dances, contact the Indian Pueblo Cultural Center, 2401 12th Street NW, Albuquerque, New Mexico 87103, and the Hopi Cultural Center, P.O. Box 67, Second Mesa, Arizona 86043.

SOURCES OF MORE TECHNICAL INFORMATION

Ambler, J. Richard. *The Anasazi.* Flagstaff, Arizona: Museum of Northern Arizona Press, 1977. Authoritative text and excellent color photos of artifacts.

Bandelier, Adolph F. *The Delight Makers.* New York: Harcourt, Brace, Jovanovich, 1890. A novel about Anasazi life at Bandelier National Monument, New Mexico, by a pioneer archaeologist.

Green, Jesse, ed. *Zuni: Selected Writings of Frank Hamilton Cushing.* Lincoln: University of Nebraska Press, 1979. Wonderful stories about traditional Zuni life by a pioneer Anglo anthropologist initiated into Zuni religion.

Jones, Dewitt, and Linda S. Cordell. *Anasazi World.* Portland, Oregon: Graphic Arts Center, 1985. Spectacular photographs of ruins and authoritative text.

Lister, Robert H. and Florence C. *Those Who Came Before: Southwestern Archaeology in the National Park System.* Tucson, Arizona: Southwest Parks and Monuments Association, 1983. A good guide to Anasazi ruins preserved in national parks, and a summary of Southwestern archaeology.

Matlock, Gary. *Enemy Ancestors: The Anasazi World with a Guide to Sites.* Flagstaff, Arizona: Northland Press, 1988. One archaeologist's understanding of the Anasazi world, with fine photographs by Scott Warren, particularly of lesser-known sites.

Noble, David Grant. *New Light on Chaco Canyon.* Santa Fe, New Mexico: School of American Research Press, 1984. Summarizes the most current information about Chaco culture.

Simmons, Leo W. *Sun Chief: The Autobiography of a Hopi Indian.* New Haven, Connecticut: Yale University Press, 1942. One Hopi man's life, including descriptions of traditional farming, weddings, and ceremonies.

▲▲▲▲▲▲▲▲▲▲▲▲▲▲▲▲▲▲▲▲▲▲▲▲▲▲▲

CHILDREN'S BOOKS

Bleeker, Sonia. *The Pueblo Indians: Farmers of the Rio Grande.* New York: William Morrow, 1955. Classic story, with named characters.

Elting, Mary, and Michael Folsom. *The Secret Story of Pueblo Bonito.* New York: Scholastic Book Services, 1963. The story of the peo-

ple who lived in the "Canyon of Great
Houses."

Erdoes, Richard. *The Rain Dance People: The
Pueblo Indians, Their Past and Present.* New
York: Alfred A. Knopf, 1976. Authoritative
and informative.

Marriott, Alice. *The First Comers: Indians of
America's Dawn.* New York: Longmans,
Green, 1960. Introduction to all North
American prehistory, with extensive
descriptions of how archaeologists do
their work.

Paul, Paula G. *Dance With Me, Gods.* New York:
Lodestar Books/E. P. Dutton, 1982. A novel
about the Pueblo revolt against the Spanish
in 1680.

Tamarin, Alfred, and Shirley Glubok. *Ancient
Indians of the Southwest.* Garden City, New
York: Doubleday and Company, 1975. Information on all the major prehistoric Southwest cultures.

Wood, Nancy and Myron. *Hollering Sun.* New
York: Simon and Schuster, 1972. Poetic
impressions of modern Taos Pueblo, with
black-and-white photographs.

Yue, David and Charlotte. *The Pueblo.* Boston:
Houghton Mifflin, 1986. A summary of
Anasazi and Pueblo lifeways.

GLOSSARY

Anasazi   The prehistoric Southwestern people
who lived in the area where Utah, Colorado,
New Mexico, and Arizona meet. They farmed
and lived in pueblos made from stone, and the
ruins of those pueblos can still be seen in
national parks like Mesa Verde in Colorado and
lesser-known places like Navajo National Monument in Arizona. *Anasazi* means "someone's
ancestors" in Navajo.

artifact   Anything made by human beings.

ash mound   Where fireplace ashes, corncobs,
and broken pottery and tools were discarded at
the edge of a village. Burials were often made
there, and it is a good place for archaeologists to
excavate.

Big River Village/Aztec Ruins   In the story, the
people of the Village of Blue Stone call this
nearby village "Big River Village." Its modern
name is Aztec Ruins, a large Chaco Culture village with 405 rooms and 28 kivas. Today, it is a
national monument near Aztec, New Mexico,
with a spectacular reconstructed great kiva.
Aztec is an Anasazi ruin with no connection to
the Aztecs of Mexico. Pioneers named it before

the Anasazi were recognized as the builders of such villages.

Canyon of Great Houses/Chaco Canyon   In the late 1000s and early 1100s, the Anasazi reached their first great cultural peak in a desolate area of northwestern New Mexico. Five thousand small villages (like the Village of Blue Stone) and nearly one hundred large towns, many of them connected by prehistoric roads, were built across thousands of square miles. The center of this culture was Chaco Canyon, where today the magnificent ruins are protected in Chaco Culture National Historic Park. The biggest Chaco Canyon village is Pueblo Bonito, which contains more than six hundred rooms.

clan   Your clan is your identity and determines much of your loyalty; whom you can marry (only someone of another clan); which ceremonies you will participate in; and the homes and fields you will use (since the women of clans own houses and land). Clans are even more important than family. Modern Pueblo people at the villages of Hopi, Zuni, and Acoma are born into their mothers' clans, and archaeologists assume that Anasazi people were, too.

Corn Mother   A perfect ear of white corn, the symbolic mother of all Anasazi and Pueblo people. A Corn Mother is given to a child as its first present at birth.

fetish   A carved or natural object that represents the spirit of an animal or power. Animal fetishes help in hunting and healing. Other more abstract fetishes represent fertility or good crops or anything its owner has faith in. Fetishes are carried with respect in a pouch called a medicine bag.

jet   A kind of hard, black coal used for carvings and jewelry.

kiva   A ceremonial chamber, usually underground, used mostly by men.

mano   The stone held in the hand and used to grind corn or seeds in a metate.

mesa   A flat-topped mountain formed by erosion of a plateau. Mesas are wider than they are tall. When they erode even more, they become buttes—taller than they are wide. Eventually, only a spire or monument remains, and then it erodes away completely.

metate   The trough, made from a slab of rock, in which corn is ground with a mano. Anasazi and Pueblo women use a series of metates, each one finer-grained, to grind their corn finer and finer.

Navajo Indian people who migrated south from Alaska and Canada in about 1400, moving into the Southwest where the Pueblo people had lived for centuries. Traditionally, Navajo people are nomadic, herding sheep they acquired from the Spanish in the 1500s.

Old Clay Woman The guiding spirit of potters. Old Clay Woman taught the Anasazi how to make pottery long ago, and when Pueblo women make pottery now, they still pray to Old Clay Woman for protection and inspiration.

piki A very thin corn bread made from thin blue cornmeal batter cooked quickly on a hot stone. The parchmentlike sheets are usually rolled after cooking.

pot hunter A person who vandalizes ancient ruins, digging for artifacts to sell.

prayer stick A stick with a turkey or eagle feather attached. It carries the prayers of the person who made it. A downy breast feather from an eagle attached to a cotton string symbolizes the breath of life.

pueblo A Spanish word that means "village." The word refers to the stone and adobe villages of Anasazi and Pueblo people, and to the people who build and live in these towns. Modern Pueblo Indians are the direct descendants of the Anasazi.

sherd A fragment from a broken pot. Also called *potsherd*.

sipapu A small hole in the floor of a kiva, representing the Place of Emergence into this world.

temper The finely ground powder (made from old potsherds or sand or volcanic ash) added to clay when making pottery to keep it from cracking during drying and firing.

Village of Blue Stone An imaginary Anasazi village located in the mesas north of Aztec Ruins. Though not a real village, this pueblo resembles the dozens of small pueblos that surrounded a major Chaco Culture village like Aztec.

yucca A spiky-leaved plant that grows all over the Southwest. Fibers from its leaves can be used for making baskets, sandals, twine, paintbrushes, and many other tools. Its roots make soapy suds in water and are used as shampoo and in purifying rituals by many Southwest Indian peoples.

INDEX

▲▲▲▲▲▲▲▲▲▲▲▲▲▲▲▲▲▲▲▲▲▲▲▲▲▲▲